Panini Sandwich Recipes

51 Quick & Easy, Delicious Panini Sandwich Recipes for the Busy Person Using a Panini Press Grill

Table of Contents

Introduction...2

The Recipes..5

Ham & Havarti Melt 6

Smoked Caprese Panini..........................8

Grilled Pesto Chicken Panini...............10

Bacon and Pear with Bleu Cheese Croissant......12

Mushroom & Onion Sourdough Panini.............14

Chorizo-Apple & Arugula Panini 16

Pepper Jack BBQ Chicken Sliders.....................18

Spicy Turkey Cream Cheese Panini...................20

Chicken Panini with Southwest Aioli.................22

Rueben with a Twist Panini 24

Roast Beef with Horseradish and Smoked Gouda Panini 26

Tuna Salad Melt..28

Brie with Fig and Prosciutto on Focaccia...........30

Creamy Ham-Raspberry Stackers 32

Classic Turkey & Swiss with Basil Panini..........34

Grilled Asparagus with Bacon and Havarti Panini 36

Tomato-Basil & Mozzarella Panini....................38

Grilled Honey & Ham Cheesy Panini 40

Creamy Orange & Sausage with Basil Croissant42

Greek Panini with Yogurt & Sundried Tomatoes44

Grilled Peach with Goat Cheese and Greens Panini
....46

Southwest Chicken and Red Pepper Quesadilla 48

Pastrami with Swiss, Mushrooms & Spinach 50

Chocolate Hazelnut with Berries & Vanilla Cream
Panini 52

Pancetta with Gouda & Red Pepper Aioli Panini54

Southwest Pulled Pork Panini 56

Creamy Spinach Melt...58

Grilled Zucchini with Smoked Mozzarella Panini60

Beef Stackers with Grilled Vegetables 62

Blackened Salmon with Capers Panini...............64

Minty Strawberry-Mango Croissant 66

Grilled Portabella with Gruyere Panini 68

Almond Butter with Honey, Apples & Pecans
Panini 70

Herbed Two-Meat Panini.....................................72

Mexican Stackers 74

Chipotle Beef with Monterey Jack Panini..........76

Chicken with Avocado & Colby Jack Panini 78

Smoked Sausage with Grilled Peppers & Onions Panini 80

Piled High Vegetable Panini 82

Chicken & Grape Salad Panini 84

Creamy Herbed Roast Beef Panini 86

Chocolate Nut S'mores Croissant 88

Red Chile Chicken & Bacon Panini 90

Chili with Onions & Cheddar Panini...................92

Italian Pizza Panini...94

Classic Cheeseburger Panini...............................96

Bacon with Jalapeño & Pineapple Panini...........98

Savory Ham with Dates & Brie Panini 100

Turkey with Roasted Red Pepper & Goat Cheese Panini 102

Banana Bread with Strawberries Panini 104

Philly Cheese Steak Panini................................106

ABOUT THE AUTHOR 109

Introduction

"I don't need music, lobster or wine

Whenever your eyes look into mine;

The things I long for are simple and few:

A cup of coffee, a sandwich – and you!"

- Billy Rose (American Composer)

The term Panini comes from Panino, an Italian word that describes a sandwich made from rolls, buns or any bread that is not sliced. The American Panini sandwich was adapted from the Italian version and refers to a sandwich that has been pressed or toasted.

Sandwiches are a tasty, satisfying way to create a fast, nutritious meal, as many people are on the go most of the time and need something they can throw together quickly.

The Panini sandwich recipes in this book are the ideal solution to fast meals and nutritious food. They're quick and easy, full of the nutrients your body can use, and are delicious to boot!

Panini sandwich makers are a very convenient way to create wonderful pressed sandwiches. Units vary in size, capabilities and price. Features include capabilities such as: grill surface size, adjustable thermostat, floating hinge or adjustable height control (for adjusting to sandwich height), removable plates (for easy clean up), and drainage features (which allow drainage of fats or oils when grilling poultry, meats, etc.)

The recipes in this book are geared toward smaller units that cost less – between $20 - $50 – and have fewer features than more expensive units.

Tips for using your Panini press:

Heating:

Some units have a temperature gauge, and some have merely an on/off switch. The heat suggested for the recipes in this book is medium/high, as that setting will give a great end product. However, depending on the unit, you may have to adjust cooking times a bit to get your sandwiches cooked perfectly.

Don't Smash:

Panini grills often times come with an adjustable floating hinge that adjusts to the size of your sandwich. Just close the cover and let it rest on top of the sandwich – don't try to flatten it or you may wind up with a mess!

Easy Clean-up:

Depending on the unit you have, you may be able to remove the plates for easy clean-up. If not, you can clean the grill plates with a scratch-resistant scrubber and cloth. Note: Always wait until unit is completely cool before cleaning.

The Recipes

Ham & Havarti Melt

4 slices crusty white bread

Butter

Mayonnaise

Dijon mustard

2 slices tomato

2 slices honey spiral ham

2 slices havarti cheese

Preheat Panini grill to med-high heat. Butter one side of all 4 slices of bread. On the other side, spread a light layer of mayonnaise and Dijon mustard. Set 2 slices, butter side down, on a clean surface. Layer tomato, ham and cheese on top of each. Cover with remaining 2 slices of bread, butter side up. Place sandwiches on grill.

Close grill lid and cook for 4 – 5 minutes or until

cheese is melted. Remove each sandwich from grill and serve immediately.

Easy Side Dish: Canned tomato soup, warmed.

Serves: 2

Smoked Caprese Panini

4 slices French bread

Extra virgin olive oil

Tomato slices

Sea salt and pepper

Smoked mozzarella slices

A few fresh basil leaves

Preheat Panini grill to med-high heat. Lightly brush olive oil on one side of each slice of French bread. Place 2 slices, oil side down, on a clean surface. Layer a few tomatoes on each, then salt and pepper them. Add a few slices of smoked mozzarella and a few basil leaves on top of each. Cover with other 2 slices of bread, oil side up. Place sandwiches on preheated grill.

Close grill lid and cook for 4 – 5 minutes or until sandwiches are heated through and cheese is

melted. Remove from grill and serve.

Easy Side Dish: Blueberry yogurt topped with grapes.

Serves: 2

Grilled Pesto Chicken Panini

4 slices multigrain bread

Store bought garlic infused olive oil

1 – 2 Tbsp. store bought pesto

Tomato slices

A few sliced black olives

2 precooked chicken breasts

2 slices provolone cheese

Preheat Panini grill to med-high heat. Lightly brush one side of all 4 bread slices with the garlic olive oil. Spread pesto on the other side of 2 slices and set them, oil side down, onto a clean surface. Layer tomatoes, olives, chicken breast and cheese on top of each. Cover with other 2 bread slices, oil side up. Place both sandwiches on grill.

Close grill lid and cook for 4 – 5 minutes or until sandwiches are heated through and cheese is

melted. Carefully remove from grill, cut in half and serve.

Easy Side Dish: Cucumber and tomato slices, sprinkled with sea salt and pepper.

Serves: 2

Bacon and Pear with Bleu Cheese Croissant

2 medium croissants, sliced in half, lengthwise

1 Tbsp. bleu cheese dressing

4 slices bacon

A few pear slices

Romaine lettuce leaves

Bleu cheese crumbles

Preheat Panini grill to med-high heat. Spread bleu cheese dressing on the bottom halves of both croissants, and then place them on a clean surface, dressing side up. Layer the bacon, pear slices and lettuce on top of each. Sprinkle a few bleu cheese crumbles over all. Top with other croissant halves and place on grill.

Close grill lid and cook for 4 – 5 minutes or until sandwiches are heated through. Carefully remove from grill and serve.

Easy Side Dish: Fruit slices such as pear and apple, paired with cheddar cheese slices.

Serves: 2

Mushroom & Onion Sourdough Panini

4 slices thick sourdough bread

Butter

1 cup sliced fresh mushrooms

½ small onion, sliced in thin strips

1 tsp. butter

1 tsp. olive oil

Sea salt and pepper

2 slices Swiss cheese

Preheat Panini grill to med-high heat. Butter one side of each slice of bread. Place mushrooms and onion in a small skillet with the butter and olive oil. Sauté over medium heat until the vegetables are lightly browned. Season to taste with sea salt and pepper.

Place 2 slices bread, butter side down onto a clean surface and spoon mushroom/onion mixture on top. Add Swiss cheese and other slice of bread, butter side up, on each. Place both sandwiches on preheated grill.

Close the grill lid and cook for 4 – 5 minutes or until cheese is melted. Remove from grill, slice into halves and serve.

Easy Side Dish: Store bought nut mixture sprinkled with chili powder.

Serves: 2

Chorizo-Apple & Arugula Panini

4 slices white bread

Olive oil

Mayonnaise

Yellow mustard

A few slices chorizo sausage

A few apple slices

2 slices cheddar cheese

Arugula lettuce leaves

Preheat Panini grill to med-high heat. Lightly brush olive oil on one side of each slice of bread. On the other side of 2 slices, spread a light layer of mayonnaise and mustard, and place them on a clean surface, oil side down. Layer the chorizo, apple slices, cheese and arugula leaves on top of each. Cover with other 2 slices of bread, oil side up. Place both sandwiches on grill.

Close grill lid and cook for 4 – 5 minutes or until sandwiches are heated through and cheese is melted. Remove from grill and serve.

Easy Side Dish: Crackers with store-bought cheese ball.

Serves: 2

Pepper Jack BBQ Chicken Sliders

4 small slider buns, split

1 cup shredded chicken (from store-bought rotisserie chicken)

¼ cup barbecue sauce

A few spicy, pickled pepper rings

2 slices Pepper Jack cheese, cut in half

Preheat Panini grill to med-high heat. In a small bowl combine shredded chicken and barbecue sauce; stir well. Place a spoonful of meat onto the bottom half of each slider bun, and set on a clean surface. Place some pepper rings and a slice of Pepper Jack cheese on each. Top with other bun halves and place each sandwich on the grill.

Close grill lid and cook for 4 – 5 minutes or until buns are hot and cheese is melted. Remove from grill and serve immediately.

Easy Side Dish: Mixed salad greens with a few pickled pepper rings on top.

Serves: 2

Spicy Turkey Cream Cheese Panini

8 baguette rounds

1 – 2 Tbsp. cream cheese

2 Tbsp. canned cranberry sauce

4 slices deli turkey, sliced in half

1 jalapeño, seeded and sliced in thin rings

2 slices havarti cheese, sliced in half

Preheat Panini grill to med-high heat. Spread cream cheese and cranberry sauce on 4 baguette rounds and place on a clean surface, cream cheese side up. Layer the turkey, jalapeño rings and havarti cheese on top of each. Top with other baguette rounds and place on grill.

Close grill lid and cook for 4 – 5 minutes or until rounds are heated through and cheese is melted. Remove from grill and enjoy!

Easy Side Dish: Salad of romaine lettuce, shredded parmesan and Caesar dressing.

Serves: 2

Chicken Panini with Southwest Aioli

4 slices crusty white bread

1 Tbsp. mayonnaise

1 tsp. fresh lemon juice

1 tsp. taco seasoning

Dash of garlic powder

2 pre-grilled chicken breasts

Avocado slices

Shredded iceberg lettuce

2 slices Monterey Jack cheese

Preheat Panini grill to med-high heat. In a bowl, mix together mayonnaise, lemon juice, taco seasoning and garlic powder; spread on one side of each slice of bread. Set 2 slices, aioli side up onto a clean surface. Place chicken breasts, avocado slices, lettuce and cheese on top of each. Top with other 2 slices of bread, aioli side down. Place both sandwiches on grill.

Close grill lid and cook for 4 – 5 minutes or until sandwiches are heated through and cheese is melted. Remove from grill and enjoy!

Easy Side Dish: Salsa made of tomatoes, onion, bell pepper, a splash of red wine vinegar, sea salt and pepper; served with tortilla chips.

Serves: 2

Rueben with a Twist Panini

4 slices dark rye bread

Butter

1 Tbsp. Thousand Island dressing

1 Tbsp. sweet pickle relish

7 – 8 oz. corned beef

¼ cup sauerkraut

2 slices Swiss cheese

Preheat Panini grill to med-high heat. Butter all 4 slices of bread. Spread Thousand Island dressing and sweet pickle relish on the other side of 2 slices and place on a clean surface, butter side down. Layer the corned beef, sauerkraut and Swiss cheese on top of each. Top with other slices of rye bread, butter side up and place on grill.

Close grill lid and cook for 4 – 5 minutes or until sandwiches are heated through and cheese is

melted. Carefully remove each from grill, slice in half and serve.

Easy Side Dish: Sour cream mixed with dry onion soup mix; served with potato chips.

Serves: 2

Roast Beef with Horseradish and Smoked Gouda Panini

4 slices crusty French bread

Butter

1 Tbsp. sour cream

2 tsp. hot horseradish

4 slices tomato

4 slices deli roast beef

2 slices smoked Gouda cheese

Preheat Panini grill to med-high heat. Spread butter on one side of all 4 slices of bread. Mix together sour cream and horseradish, spread on the other side of 2 bread slices and place on a clean cutting board, butter side down. Layer the tomatoes, roast beef and Gouda cheese on top of each. Top with other French bread slices, butter side up and place both sandwiches on grill.

Close grill lid and cook for 4 – 5 minutes or until

cheese is melted and sandwiches are hot. Remove from grill and enjoy!

Easy Side Dish: Easy fruit salad of pineapple, banana slices and grapes, drizzled with honey.

Serves: 2

Tuna Salad Melt

4 slices wheat bread

Butter

1 – 6 oz. can of tuna, packed in water, drained

1 Tbsp. mayonnaise

1 Tbsp. salad dressing (such as Miracle Whip)

2 tsp. yellow mustard

1 Tbsp. finely diced dill pickles

1 Tbsp. finely diced celery

¼ cup shredded cheddar cheese

Preheat Panini grill to med-high heat. Butter one side of all 4 slices of bread. In a bowl, combine the tuna, mayonnaise, salad dressing, mustard, pickles, celery and cheese; mix well. Spread some of the tuna mixture on the non-buttered side of 2 slices of bread place and place the other 2 slices of bread on top, butter side up. Place both sandwiches on grill.

Close grill lid and cook for 4 – 5 minutes or until cheese is melted. Remove from grill and enjoy!

Easy Side Dish: Bottled organic applesauce, sprinkled with ground cinnamon.

Serves: 2

Brie with Fig and Prosciutto on Focaccia

2 medium squares of focaccia bread, sliced in half lengthwise

1 Tbsp. fig preserves

6 thin slices prosciutto

A few slices brie cheese

Butter lettuce leaves

Preheat Panini grill to med-high heat. Spread the fig preserves on both bottom halves of focaccia and place on clean surface, fig side up. Layer prosciutto, brie and lettuce leaves on both; top with other focaccia halves and place on grill.

Close grill lid and cook for 4 – 5 minutes or until bread is warm and brie is melted. Carefully remove from grill and enjoy!

Easy Side Dish: Store-bought spinach artichoke dip served with crackers.

Serves: 2

Creamy Ham-Raspberry Stackers

8 small baguette rounds

1 – 2 Tbsp. cream cheese

1 Tbsp. raspberry jam

2 slices ham deli meat, sliced in half

2 slices havarti cheese, sliced in half

Preheat Panini grill to med-high heat. Spread cream cheese and raspberry jam on 4 baguette rounds and place on a clean surface, jam side up. Layer the ham and havarti cheese on each and top with other baguette rounds. Place each sandwich on grill.

Close grill lid and cook for 4 – 5 minutes or until rounds are heated through and cheese is melted. Remove from grill and enjoy immediately!

Easy Side Dish: Vanilla yogurt topped with fresh

berries of choice.

Serves: 2

Classic Turkey & Swiss with Basil Panini

2 seeded buns, split

1 – 2 Tbsp. mayonnaise

4 slices deli turkey

4 slices fresh tomato

2 slices Swiss cheese

A few fresh basil leaves

Preheat Panini grill to med-high heat. Spread the mayonnaise on both bottom bun halves and place on a clean surface. Layer turkey, tomato, cheese and basil leaves on top of each and top with other bun halves. Place each sandwich on grill.

Close grill lid and cook for 4 – 5 minutes or until sandwiches are hot and cheese is melted. Carefully remove both sandwiches and serve.

Easy Side Dish: Fresh carrot and celery sticks with ranch dressing for dipping.

Serves: 2

Grilled Asparagus with Bacon and Havarti Panini

6 asparagus spears, washed and trimmed

Butter

Sea salt and pepper

4 slices white bread

4 slices precooked bacon

2 slices havarti cheese

Preheat Panini grill to med-high heat. Toss asparagus spears in butter, sea salt and pepper; place on grill for 3 – 4 minutes, turning once during cooking time. Remove asparagus and set aside.

Butter one side of all 4 slices of bread. Place 2 slices, butter side down onto a clean surface and place grilled asparagus, bacon and havarti cheese on top of each. Top with other bread slices, butter side up and place sandwiches on grill.

Close grill lid and cook for 4 – 5 minutes or until sandwiches are heated through and cheese is melted. Remove from grill and serve.

Easy Side Dish: Apple slices and orange sections, dipped in yogurt whipped with cream cheese.

Serves: 2

Tomato-Basil & Mozzarella Panini

4 slices thick, crusty white bread

Store bought garlic infused olive oil

4 slices tomato

3 – 4 slices fresh mozzarella

A few fresh basil leaves

A few drops of balsamic vinegar

Sea salt and pepper

Preheat Panini grill to med-high heat. Lightly brush one side of each slice of bread with the garlic olive oil. Place 2 slices, oil side down on a clean cutting board. Layer tomatoes, mozzarella slices and basil leaves on top of each. Sprinkle with balsamic vinegar, sea salt and pepper. Top with other bread slices, oil side up and place each sandwich on grill.

Close grill lid and cook for 4 – 5 minutes or until cheese is melted. Remove sandwiches, cut in half and serve.

Easy Side Dish: Small antipasto plate of kalamata olives, marinated artichoke hearts and mozzarella balls.

Serves: 2

Grilled Honey & Ham Cheesy Panini

4 slices French bread

Butter

6 oz. shaved deli ham

2 slices cheddar cheese

2 – 3 tsp. honey

Preheat Panini grill to med-high heat. Butter one side of each slice of bread. Place 2 slices, butter side down on a clean surface and layer ham and cheese on top of each. Drizzle with honey. Top with other 2 bread slices, butter side up and place on grill.

Close grill lid and cook for 4 – 5 minutes or until cheese is melted. Carefully remove sandwiches, cut in half and serve.

Easy Side Dish: Canned vegetable soup, warmed.

Serves: 2

Creamy Orange & Sausage with Basil Croissant

2 medium croissants, sliced in half lengthwise

1 Tbsp. cream cheese

1 Tbsp. orange marmalade

Sliced precooked sausage

2 slices provolone cheese

A few basil leaves

Preheat Panini grill to med-high heat. Spread cream cheese and orange marmalade on both bottom croissant halves. Place on clean surface, cream cheese side up. Layer sausage, provolone cheese and basil leaves on top of each and cover with croissant tops. Place each sandwich on grill.

Close grill lid and cook for 4 – 5 minutes or until sandwiches are warm and cheese is melted. Remove sandwiches, cut in half and serve.

Easy Side Dish: Sliced raw vegetable medley, with bleu cheese dressing for dipping.

Serves: 2

Greek Panini with Yogurt & Sundried Tomatoes

4 pocketless pitas

1 Tbsp. plain yogurt

Sea salt and pepper

Cucumber slices

Tomato slices

Red onion slices

2 Tbsp. chopped sundried tomatoes

Feta cheese

Chopped fresh parsley

Preheat Panini grill to med-high heat. Spread the yogurt on two pitas. Sprinkle sea salt and pepper over yogurt and place both pitas on a clean surface, yogurt side up. Layer cucumber slices, tomato slices and red onion on both. Sprinkle sundried tomatoes, feta cheese and parsley on top. Cover with other 2 pitas and place on preheated grill.

Close grill lid and cook for 4 – 5 minutes or until sandwiches are warmed through. Remove sandwiches, cut in half and serve.

Easy Side Dish: Store bought yogurt dip with rice crackers.

Serves: 2

Grilled Peach with Goat Cheese and Greens Panini

1 medium peach, pitted and cut in half

4 slices country style bread

Butter

Plain goat cheese

Mixed salad greens

Basil leaves

Preheat Panini grill to med-high heat. Place both peach halves, cut side down onto grill and let cook for about 4 minutes.

Meanwhile, butter one side of all 4 slices of bread. Spread the goat cheese on the other side of 2 slices and place on a clean surface, cheese side up. Remove the peach halves from the grill and slice in thin strips. Layer slices of peaches on top of goat cheese, then layer salad greens and basil leaves on top of each. Cover with other 2 slices of bread, butter side up. Place both sandwiches on grill.

Close the grill lid and cook for 4 – 5 minutes or until sandwiches are warm and cheese is melted. Carefully remove sandwiches and serve.

Easy Side Dish: Fresh chunks of mozzarella, chopped tomatoes and chopped basil leaves, mixed together with a dash of balsamic vinegar, sea salt and pepper. Serve with baguette rounds.

Serves: 2

Southwest Chicken and Red Pepper Quesadilla

2 medium flour tortillas

Butter

½ cup shredded cheddar cheese

Precooked chicken strips

½ medium red bell pepper, sliced in thin strips

½ tsp. chili powder

¼ tsp. ground cumin

Chopped fresh cilantro

Preheat Panini grill to med-high heat. Butter one side of both tortillas. Place one tortilla, butter side down on a clean surface. Sprinkle cheddar cheese on top. Next, scatter chicken strips and bell pepper strips over the cheese. Sprinkle chili powder, cumin and cilantro on top. Cover with other tortilla, butter side up and carefully place quesadilla on grill.

Close the grill lid and cook for 3 – 4 minutes or until cheese is melted. Carefully remove quesadilla, cut into quarters and serve.

Easy Side Dish: In a bowl, mash 1 avocado and mix with 1 chopped tomato, chopped cilantro, and ranch dressing mix to taste. Serve with tortilla chips.

Serves: 2

Pastrami with Swiss, Mushrooms & Spinach

4 slices sourdough bread

Store bought garlic infused olive oil

1 cup sliced fresh mushrooms

½ small onion, thinly sliced

1 Tbsp. butter

Sea salt and pepper

8 oz. deli pastrami

2 slices Swiss cheese

Baby spinach leaves

Preheat Panini grill to med-high heat. Lightly brush the garlic olive oil on one side of all 4 slices of sourdough bread. In a small skillet, sauté the mushrooms and onion in butter until onions are translucent; season with sea salt and pepper. Place

2 slices of bread onto clean surface, oil side down. Pile mushroom/onion mixture and pastrami on top of both; next layer Swiss cheese and spinach leaves. Top with other 2 bread slices, oil side up. Place both sandwiches on preheated grill.

Close the grill lid and cook for 4 – 5 minutes or until sandwiches are warm and cheese is melted. Remove sandwiches from grill, cut in half and serve.

Easy Side Dish: Jalapeño preserves poured over cream cheese and serve with crackers.

Serves: 2

Chocolate Hazelnut with Berries & Vanilla Cream Panini

4 slices country style bread

Butter

1 – 2 Tbsp. chocolate hazelnut spread

¼ cup fresh mixed berries

½ cup heavy whipping cream

2 Tbsp. sugar

½ tsp. vanilla extract

Preheat Panini grill to med-high heat. Butter one side of all 4 slices of bread. Spread chocolate hazelnut spread onto the other side of 2 slices and place them on a clean surface, butter side down. Sprinkle berries on top and cover with remaining bread slices, butter side up. Place both sandwiches on grill.

Close the grill lid and cook for 4 – 5 minutes or until sandwiches are warmed through.

While sandwiches are cooking, pour whipping cream into a small bowl. Add sugar and vanilla and beat with an electric mixer for 1 – 2 minutes or until cream becomes thick.

Remove sandwiches from grill and slice in half. Serve with whipped vanilla cream for dipping.

Easy Side Dish: Fruit salad mixture of berries, pineapple, banana and grapes, sprinkled with lemon juice and a dash of sugar.

Serves: 2

Pancetta with Gouda & Red Pepper Aioli Panini

6 thin strips of pancetta

4 slices rustic white bread

Store bought garlic infused olive oil

2 Tbsp. mayonnaise

1 Tbsp. finely diced red bell peppers

1 tsp. fresh lemon juice

Sea salt and pepper

Fresh tomato slices

2 slices Gouda cheese

Preheat oven broiler. Lay pancetta on a baking sheet and place under broiler, turning once during cooking time, for about 8 minutes or until crispy. Remove from oven and lay on paper towel to drain.

Preheat Panini grill to med-high heat. Lightly brush the garlic olive oil on one side of all 4 slices of bread. In a small bowl, combine mayonnaise, diced red bell peppers and lemon juice; whisk together and season with sea salt and pepper. Spread some of the aioli on the other side of 2 slices of bread and place on a clean surface, aioli side up. Layer cooked pancetta, tomato slices and Gouda cheese on top. Cover with other 2 bread slices, oil side up. Place both sandwiches onto grill.

Close the grill lid and cook for 4 – 5 minutes or until cheese is melted. Remove from grill, cut in half and serve.

Easy Side Dish: Spinach salad containing spinach leaves, red onion, strawberries and pecans, drizzled with store bought poppy seed dressing.

Serves: 2

Southwest Pulled Pork Panini

2 seeded buns

1 cup precooked shredded pork

½ cup barbecue sauce

½ cup shredded iceberg lettuce

A few pickled pepperoncinis

2 slices cheddar cheese

Preheat Panini grill to med-high heat. In a small bowl, mix together shredded pork and barbecue sauce. Place bottom bun halves on a clean surface and pile both with barbecued pork. Put shredded lettuce, a few pepperoncini rings and cheddar cheese on top. Cover with bun tops and place on grill.

Close the grill lid and cook for 4 – 5 minutes or until sandwiches are warm and cheese is melted. Remove sandwiches from grill and serve.

Easy Side Dish: Finely chop some pepperoncinis and mix with cottage cheese. Serve with potato chips.

Serves: 2

Creamy Spinach Melt

2 tsp. butter

1 – 10 oz. package chopped frozen spinach, thawed, with liquid squeezed out

2 Tbsp. cream cheese

2 Tbsp. mayonnaise

¼ cup shredded parmesan cheese

Sea salt and pepper

Store bought garlic infused olive oil

4 slices crusty white bread

Melt butter in a medium skillet over medium-high heat. Add spinach, cream cheese and mayonnaise and cook for about 5 minutes, or until cream cheese is melted. Stir in parmesan cheese and season with sea salt and pepper.

Preheat Panini grill to med-high heat. Lightly

brush one side of each slice of bread with the garlic olive oil. Place 2 slices, oil side down onto a clean surface. Pile spinach mixture onto both slices. Top with other 2 slices of bread, oil side up and place both sandwiches on grill.

Close the grill lid and cook for 4 – 5 minutes or until sandwiches are warmed through. Remove both sandwiches and enjoy!

Easy Side Dish: Create mini kabobs using long toothpicks and a variety of vegetables, cheese chunks and olives.

Serves: 2

Grilled Zucchini with Smoked Mozzarella Panini

1 small zucchini, sliced in half lengthwise

Olive oil

Sea salt and pepper

4 slices multigrain crusty bread

Butter

Red onion slices

4 slices smoked mozzarella cheese

Preheat Panini grill to med-high heat. Toss zucchini halves with olive oil, sea salt and pepper. Place both halves on preheated grill, cut side down and let cook for about 5 minutes.

Meanwhile, butter one side of each slice of bread. As soon as zucchini is grilled to desired consistency, remove and cut into slices. Place 2 bread slices, butter side down on a clean surface. Layer slices of zucchini, red onion and mozzarella cheese on top. Cover with remaining bread slices, butter side up and place sandwiches on grill.

Close the grill lid and cook for 4 – 5 minutes or until sandwiches are warm and cheese is melted. Remove sandwiches, slice in half and serve.

Easy Side Dish: Using hard boiled eggs from breakfast, cut in half and scoop the yolks into a small bowl. Mix with mayonnaise, Dijon mustard, paprika and parsley flakes. Spoon yolk mixture into each egg white half.

Serves: 2

Beef Stackers with Grilled Vegetables

½ small onion, cut in thin strips

½ bell pepper, cut in thin strips

½ cup sliced fresh mushrooms

2 tsp. olive oil

1 tsp. garlic and herb seasoning

8 small baguette rounds

Store bought garlic infused olive oil

1 Tbsp. sour cream

1 tsp. hot horseradish

6 – 8 oz. deli roast beef

2 slices provolone cheese, cut in half

Preheat Panini grill to med-high heat. In a bowl

combine onion, peppers, mushrooms, olive oil and seasoning; toss to coat and pour out onto preheated grill. Let cook for about 5 minutes, stirring a couple times. Remove and set aside.

Lightly brush the garlic olive oil on one side of each baguette round. Mix together the sour cream and horseradish and spread on the other side of baguettes. Place 4 rounds, oil side down onto a clean surface. Top each with grilled vegetables, roast beef and provolone cheese. Cover with other 4 rounds, oil side up and place each on grill.

Close the grill lid and cook for 4 – 5 minutes or until sandwiches are warmed through. Carefully remove each sandwich and serve.

Easy Side Dish: Top cucumber rounds with chive & onion cream cheese and canned tuna.

Serves: 2

Blackened Salmon with Capers Panini

2 small, wild caught salmon fillets

Butter

Sea salt

¼ tsp. cayenne pepper

¼ tsp. cumin

¼ tsp. chili powder

4 slices crusty white bread

Store bought garlic infused olive oil

2 slices white cheddar cheese

Romaine lettuce leaves

1 Tbsp. capers

Preheat Panini grill to med-high heat. Rub butter and spices over both salmon fillets; place on preheated grill and close lid. Let cook for about 5 minutes or until fish is opaque. Remove and set aside.

Lightly brush one side of all 4 slices of bread with the garlic olive oil. Place 2 slices, oil side down onto a clean surface. Place blackened salmon, cheese, lettuce and capers on top of both. Cover with remaining bread slices, oil side up. Place both sandwiches on grill.

Close the grill lid and cook for 4 – 5 minutes or until cheese is melted. Remove sandwiches and serve.

Easy Side Dish: Stuff green and black olives with cream cheese mixed with sour cream and ranch dressing mix.

Serves: 2

Minty Strawberry-Mango Croissant

2 medium croissants, sliced in half lengthwise

2 Tbsp. strawberry flavored cream cheese

4 fresh strawberries, sliced

1 mango, pitted and sliced

A few fresh mint leaves

Preheat Panini grill to med-high heat. Spread strawberry cream cheese on both bottom halves of croissants. Place them on a clean surface, cream cheese side up. Layer strawberries, mango slices and mint leaves on top. Cover with top halves of croissants and place both sandwiches on grill.

Close the grill lid and cook for 3 – 4 minutes or until sandwiches are warm. Carefully remove from grill and serve.

Easy Side Dish: Fill endive leaves with chopped

apple and celery, and sprinkle with cinnamon.

Serves: 2

Grilled Portabella with Gruyere Panini

2 large portabella mushroom caps

4 slices sourdough or white bread

Butter

White onion slices

Spinach leaves

2 slices gruyere cheese

Preheat Panini grill to med-high heat. Place both mushroom caps on grill and cook for about 4 – 5 minutes or until done to desired consistency. Remove and set aside.

Butter one side of all 4 slices of bread. Place 2 slices, butter side down onto a clean surface. Top each with a grilled portabella cap, onion slices, spinach leaves and gruyere cheese. Cover with remaining bread slices, butter side up. Place sandwiches on grill.

Close the grill lid and cook for 4 – 5 minutes or until cheese is melted and sandwiches are warmed through. Remove from grill and serve.

Easy Side Dish: Salsa of chopped strawberries, minced jalapeño, finely chopped onion, chopped cilantro, olive oil, sea salt and pepper. Serve with tortilla chips.

Serves: 2

Almond Butter with Honey, Apples & Pecans Panini

4 slices wheat bread

Butter

1 – 2 Tbsp. almond butter

Apple slices

Whole pecans

Honey

Cinnamon

Butter one side of all 4 slices of bread. Spread almond butter on the other side of 2 slices and place on a clean surface, butter side down. Layer apple slices and pecans on the almond butter. Drizzle honey over all and sprinkle with cinnamon. Top with other 2 bread slices, butter side up and place both sandwiches on heated grill.

Close the grill lid and cook for 3 – 4 minutes or until sandwiches are warm. Remove from grill and enjoy!

Easy Side Dish: Blend together ¼ cup fresh cranberries, 1 orange, some spinach leaves and ½ cup vanilla yogurt with some ice and water for a nutritious side smoothie.

Serves: 2

Herbed Two-Meat Panini

2 large rolls or buns

1 – 2 Tbsp. herb and chive cream cheese

2 Tbsp. canned cranberry sauce

4 oz. deli turkey

4 oz. deli ham

2 slices provolone cheese

Chopped parsley

Preheat Panini grill to med-high heat. Spread herb and chive cream cheese and cranberry sauce on both bottom halves of buns. Place them on a clean surface, cream cheese side up. Layer turkey, ham and cheese on top of both. Sprinkle with parsley and cover with top bun halves. Place each sandwich on grill.

Close the grill lid and cook for 4 – 5 minutes or until sandwiches are warmed through and cheese is melted. Remove from grill and serve.

Easy Side Dish: Store bought hummus with crackers.

Serves: 2

Mexican Stackers

8 small squares of focaccia bread

1 – 2 Tbsp. store bought salsa

1 small avocado, pitted and sliced

Chorizo sausage slices

½ green bell pepper, thinly sliced

2 slices Pepper Jack cheese, cut in half

Preheat Panini grill to med-high heat. Spread the salsa on the bottom half of each piece of focaccia; place on a clean surface, salsa side up. Layer avocado, sausage slices, bell pepper and cheese on each; cover with focaccia tops and place each on grill.

Close the grill lid and cook for 3 – 4 minutes or until sandwiches are warm and cheese is melted. Remove sandwiches from grill and serve.

Easy Side Dish: Top crackers with refried beans, sliced olives and shredded cheddar cheese.

Serves: 2

Chipotle Beef with Monterey Jack Panini

4 slices Ciabatta bread

Store bought garlic infused olive oil

2 Tbsp. mayonnaise

2 tsp. finely chopped chipotle in adobo sauce

1 tsp. fresh lime juice

Sea salt and pepper

1 cup precooked shredded or deli roast beef

Butter lettuce leaves

2 slices Monterey Jack cheese

Preheat Panini grill to med-high heat. Lightly brush the garlic olive on one side of all 4 slices of Ciabatta bread. In a small bowl, mix together the mayonnaise, chopped chipotle, lime juice, sea salt and pepper to create an aioli. Spread some of the chipotle aioli on the other side of 2 slices of bread and place them on a clean surface, oil side down. Pile shredded or deli beef, lettuce leaves and cheese on top of each. Cover with other 2 slices of bread, oil side up. Place both sandwiches on grill.

Close the grill lid and cook for 4 – 5 minutes or until cheese is melted. Remove sandwiches from grill and serve.

Easy Side Dish: Fresh sliced watermelon.

Serves: 2

Chicken with Avocado & Colby Jack Panini

2 large buns, sliced in half

1 Tbsp. mayonnaise

2 precooked chicken breasts

A few avocado slices

Red onion slices

Romaine lettuce leaves

2 slices Colby Jack cheese

Preheat Panini grill to med-high heat. Spread mayonnaise on both bottom bun halves. Place them on a clean surface, mayo side up. Layer chicken, avocado, onion, lettuce and cheese on top of each. Cover with top bun halves and place on grill.

Close the grill lid and cook for 4 – 5 minutes or

until sandwiches are warm. Carefully remove from grill and serve.

Easy Side Dish: Easy shrimp cocktail. Precooked shrimp dipped in sauce of ½ cup ketchup, 2 – 3 tsp. hot horseradish, sliced green onion and 1 Tbsp. lemon juice.

Serves: 2

Smoked Sausage with Grilled Peppers & Onions Panini

½ small onion, thinly sliced

½ red bell pepper, thinly sliced

½ yellow bell pepper, thinly sliced

2 tsp. butter, melted

Sea salt and pepper

4 slices sour dough bread

Store bought garlic infused olive oil

Sliced precooked smoked sausage

2 slices Monterey Jack cheese

Preheat Panini grill to med-high heat. In a bowl combine onion, peppers, butter, sea salt and pepper; mix well. Pour onto heated grill and let cook for about 5 minutes, stirring once or twice.

Remove and set aside. Lightly brush the garlic olive oil on one side of all 4 slices of bread. Place 2 slices on a clean surface, oil side down. Pile the grilled vegetables on each, then the smoked sausage and cheese. Cover with other 2 bread slices, oil side up. Place both sandwiches on grill.

Close the grill lid and cook for 4 – 5 minutes or until sandwiches are warm and cheese is melted. Remove sandwiches from grill and serve.

Easy Side Dish: Small block of goat cheese on a plate, topped with chopped parsley, finely chopped red bell pepper, a splash of lemon juice and a drizzle of olive oil. Serve with crackers.

Serves: 2

Piled High Vegetable Panini

4 slices herbed Ciabatta bread, such as garlic & rosemary

Butter

Tomato slices

Cucumber slices

Red onion slices

Radishes, thinly sliced

Spinach leaves

Basil leaves

2 slices of Swiss cheese

Preheat Panini grill to med-high heat. Butter one side of all 4 slices of bread. Place 2 slices, butter side down on a clean surface. Layer tomato slices, cucumber slices, red onion, radish slices, spinach and basil leaves on top of each. Cover with other 2 bread slices, butter side up. Place sandwiches on grill.

Close the grill lid and cook for 4 – 5 minutes or until cheese is melted. Carefully remove sandwiches from grill and serve.

Easy Side Dish: Salad of spinach leaves, artichoke hearts, olives, feta cheese and dried cranberries; sprinkled with store bought Italian dressing.

Serves: 2

Chicken & Grape Salad Panini

1 cup cubed precooked chicken (rotisserie chicken works well for this)

2 Tbsp. mayonnaise

1 Tbsp. salad dressing (such as Miracle Whip)

2 tsp. Dijon mustard

½ cup grapes, sliced into halves

½ cup shredded cheddar cheese

4 slices multigrain bread

Butter

Preheat Panini grill to med-high heat. In a bowl, combine chicken, mayonnaise, salad dressing, Dijon mustard, grapes and cheese; mix well. Butter one side of all 4 slices of bread. Place 2 slices, butter side down onto clean surface. Pile some chicken salad on top of each. Cover with other 2 bread slices, butter side up and place both sandwiches on grill.

84

Close the grill lid and cook for 4 – 5 minutes or until sandwiches are warmed through. Remove sandwiches from grill and serve.

Easy Side Dish: Easy baked brie. Place small brie rounds on a baking sheet and top with brown sugar, butter and chopped pecans. Bake at 375° for about 15 minutes. Serve with crackers.

Serves: 2

Creamy Herbed Roast Beef Panini

4 slices crusty white bread

Store bought garlic infused olive oil

2 Tbsp. cream cheese

2 tsp. Dijon mustard

2 tsp. chopped parsley

1 tsp. chopped dill

8 oz. deli roast beef

Spinach leaves

2 slices dill havarti cheese

Preheat Panini grill to med-high heat. Lightly brush the garlic olive oil on one side of all 4 slices of bread. On the other side of 2 slices spread the cream cheese and Dijon mustard. Place slices on a clean surface, oil side down. Sprinkle parsley and dill on top. Next, layer roast beef, spinach leaves and havarti cheese. Top with other 2 bread slices, oil side up. Place sandwiches on grill.

Close the grill lid and cook for 4 – 5 minutes or until sandwiches are warmed through and cheese is melted. Remove sandwiches from grill, cut in half and serve.

Easy Side Dish: Sliced raw bell pepper, cucumber, radishes and cauliflower. Served with ranch dressing for dipping.

Serves: 2

Chocolate Nut S'mores Croissant

2 medium croissants, sliced in half lengthwise

1 Tbsp. creamy peanut butter

1 Tbsp. chocolate hazelnut spread

4 Tbsp. mini marshmallows

2 Tbsp. mini chocolate chips

Preheat Panini grill to med-high heat. Spread the peanut butter and chocolate hazelnut spread on the bottom halves of both croissants. Place them on a clean surface, nut butter side up. Sprinkle the marshmallows and chocolate chips on top of each. Cover with croissant tops and place both sandwiches on grill.

Close the grill lid and cook for 3 – 4 minutes or until sandwiches are warmed through and chocolate chips and marshmallows are melted. Carefully remove sandwiches from grill and serve.

Easy Side Dish: Sliced fresh pears sprinkled with cinnamon and chopped pecans.

Serves: 2

Red Chile Chicken & Bacon Panini

4 slices sourdough bread

Butter

Shredded chicken (from store bought rotisserie chicken)

½ cup store bought red chile sauce

4 slices precooked bacon

A few avocado slices

2 slices Monterey Jack cheese

Butter lettuce

Preheat Panini grill to med-high heat. Butter one side of all 4 slices of bread. In a bowl, combine the chicken and red chile sauce; mix until combined. Place 2 slices of bread on a clean surface, butter side down. Pile some chicken onto each. Next, layer bacon, avocado, cheese and lettuce. Cover with other 2 slices of bread, butter side up and place both sandwiches on grill.

Close the grill lid and cook for 4 – 5 minutes or until sandwiches are warm and cheese is melted. Remove sandwiches from grill and serve.

Easy Side Dish: Imitation crab mixed with mayonnaise, sea salt and pepper. Served with rice crackers.

Serves: 2

Chili with Onions & Cheddar Panini

2 large seeded buns

1 Tbsp. mayonnaise

½ cup canned meaty chili

2 Tbsp. diced onion

½ cup shredded cheddar cheese

Pickle slices

Preheat Panini grill to med-high heat. Spread mayonnaise on the bottom bun halves. Place on a clean surface, mayo side up. Spoon chili onto bun bottoms. Next, sprinkle onion and cheddar cheese on top along with a few pickle slices. Cover with bun tops and place sandwiches on grill.

Close the grill lid and cook for 4 – 5 minutes or until sandwiches are warm and cheese is melted. Remove sandwiches from grill and serve.

Easy Side Dish: Combine store bought pickled beets, chopped tomatoes and mozzarella cheese chunks. Serve with crackers.

Serves: 2

Italian Pizza Panini

4 slices crusty white bread

Store bought garlic infused olive oil

2 Tbsp. store bought marinara sauce

A few pepperoni rounds

A few salami rounds

Sliced olives

Sliced fresh mushrooms

Shredded mozzarella cheese

Preheat Panini grill to med-high heat. Lightly brush the garlic olive oil on one side of all 4 slices of bread. Place 2 slices, oil side down on a clean surface. Layer pepperoni, salami, olives, mushrooms and mozzarella cheese on each. Top with other 2 bread slices, oil side up and place each sandwich on grill.

Close the grill lid and cook for 4 – 5 minutes or until sandwiches are warm and cheese is melted. Remove sandwiches from grill and serve.

Easy Side Dish: Apricot halves, sprinkled with pieces of goat cheese, walnuts and cinnamon, drizzled with honey.

Serves: 2

Classic Cheeseburger Panini

2 large seeded buns

1 Tbsp. mayonnaise

2 tsp. yellow mustard

2 precooked hamburger patties

2 large tomato slices

Red onion slices

Pickle slices

Romaine lettuce leaves

2 slices cheddar cheese

Preheat Panini grill to med-high heat. Spread mayonnaise and mustard on both bottom bun halves. Place on clean surface, mayo side up. Layer hamburger patties, tomato, onion, pickles, lettuce and cheese on top of both. Cover with bun tops and place each sandwich on grill.

Close the grill lid and cook for 4 – 5 minutes or until sandwiches are warm and cheese is melted. Remove sandwiches from grill and serve.

Easy Side Dish: Store bought French fries, baked. Served with fry dip of ketchup, mayonnaise and a dash of barbecue sauce.

Serves: 2

Bacon with Jalapeño & Pineapple Panini

4 slices Ciabatta bread

Butter

4 slices precooked bacon

2 canned pineapple rings

1 jalapeño, seeded and sliced in thin rings

2 slices Pepper Jack cheese

Preheat Panini grill to med-high heat. Spread butter on one side of all 4 slices of bread. Place 2 slices on a clean surface, butter side down. Layer bacon, pineapple, jalapeño rings and cheese on both. Cover with other 2 bread slices, butter side up. Place both sandwiches on grill.

Close the grill lid and cook for 4 – 5 minutes or until sandwiches are warm and cheese is melted. Carefully remove sandwiches from grill, cut in half and serve.

Easy Side Dish: Precooked meatballs, simmered on stovetop with crushed pineapple, barbecue sauce and a dash of sea salt. Use toothpicks to serve.

Serves: 2

Savory Ham with Dates & Brie Panini

4 slices French bread

Butter

8 oz. thinly sliced deli ham

¼ cup chopped dates

1 Tbsp. chopped pecans or walnuts

A few brie cheese slices

Butter one side of all 4 slices of bread. Place 2 slices on clean surface, butter side down. Layer the ham, dates, nuts and brie on top of both. Cover with other 2 bread slices, butter side up. Place both sandwiches on grill.

Close the grill lid and cook for 4 – 5 minutes or until sandwiches are warm and cheese is melted. Remove sandwiches from grill, cut in half and serve.

Easy Side Dish: Stuff pitted whole dates with cream cheese, a pecan and roll in shredded coconut.

Serves: 2

Turkey with Roasted Red Pepper & Goat Cheese Panini

4 slices country style bread

Store bought garlic infused olive oil

¼ cup goat cheese

2 Tbsp. store bought (bottled) chopped roasted red peppers

8 oz. deli turkey

Butter lettuce leaves

Preheat Panini grill to med-high heat. Lightly brush one side of all 4 slices of bread with the garlic olive oil. Spread the goat cheese on the other side of 2 slices and place them, oil side down, on a clean surface. Sprinkle the roasted red pepper over the goat cheese. Next, layer the turkey and butter lettuce on both; cover with remaining bread slices, oil side up. Place sandwiches on grill.

Close the grill lid and cook for 4 – 5 minutes or

until sandwiches are warm. Remove from grill, cut in half and serve.

Easy Side Dish: Slice tomatoes and radishes on a plate. Drizzle with melted butter and sprinkle with sea salt and pepper.

Serves: 2

Banana Bread with Strawberries Panini

4 slices store bought or homemade banana bread

Butter

1 Tbsp. cream cheese

4 strawberries, sliced

1 Tbsp. finely chopped walnuts

Preheat Panini grill to med-high heat. Butter one side of all 4 slices of banana bread. Spread cream cheese on the other side of 2 slices and place on a clean surface, butter side down. Layer strawberries and walnuts on top of each and cover with other 2 banana bread slices, butter side up. Place on grill.

Close the grill lid and cook for 3 – 4 minutes or until sandwiches are warmed through. Remove from grill and serve.

Easy Side Dish: Apple slices dipped in almond butter and drizzled with honey.

Serves: 2

Philly Cheese Steak Panini

½ green bell pepper, thinly sliced

½ small onion, thinly sliced

½ cup fresh sliced mushrooms

2 tsp. butter, melted

Sea salt and pepper

2 multigrain long buns

8 – 10 oz. deli roast beef

2 slices provolone cheese

Preheat Panini grill to med-high heat. In a bowl combine the bell pepper, onion, mushrooms, butter, sea salt and pepper; mix well. Pour mixture onto grill and let cook for about 5 minutes, stirring once or twice during cooking. Remove and set aside.

Pile the 2 bottom bun halves with grilled vegetables, roast beef and cheese. Cover with top bun halves and place both sandwiches on grill.

Close the grill lid and cook for 4 – 5 minutes or until sandwiches are warmed through and cheese is melted. Remove from grill and serve.

Easy Side Dish: Create mini fruit kabobs using long toothpicks. Use chunks of pears, apple, grapes, mangos, etc. and pair with basil and mint leaves.

Serves: 2

Thank you for enjoying this cookbook!

Other books by Mandy Stephens:

Amazing Breakfast Sandwich Recipes

51 Quick & Easy, Delicious Breakfast Sandwich Recipes for the Busy Person Using a Breakfast Sandwich Maker

Available at Amazon.com

About the Author

Mandy Stephens is a busy mom who loves food! Sandwiches (any kind) are her favorite, and she enjoys testing and experimenting with different combinations and developing recipes that are healthy, yet quick and easy for the busy person.

34611216R00073

Made in the USA
San Bernardino, CA
02 June 2016